The Abortion Conflict

A Pro/Con Issue

Deanne Durrett

Enslow Publishers, Inc.

40 Industrial Road   PO Box 38
Box 398   Aldershot
Berkeley Heights, NJ 07922   Hants GU12 6BP
USA   UK

http://www.enslow.com

Copyright © 2000 by Enslow Publishers, Inc.

Library of Congress Cataloging-in-Publication Data

Durrett, Deanne, 1940–
    The abortion conflict : a pro/con issue / Deanne Durrett.
        p. cm.
    Includes bibliographical references and index.
     ISBN 0-7660-1193-3   (hard)
        1. Abortion—Juvenile literature. 2.   Pro-life movement—Juvenile
    literature. 3.   Pro-choice movement—Juvenile literature. [1.
    Abortion.] I. Title.
       HQ767 .D87   2000
       363.46'097 3—dc21   00-009105

Printed in the United States of America

10 9 8 7 6 5 4 3 2 1

To Our Readers:
All Internet addresses in this book were active and appropriate when we went to press. Any comments or suggestions can be sent by e-mail to Comments@enslow.com or to the address on the back cover.

Illustration Credits: AP/Wide World Photos, pp. 15, 22, 31, 42, 45, 49, 55.

Cover Illustration: © Corel Corporation

Contents

Chapter 1

When Abortion Was Banned

From 1899 until 1973, abortion was illegal in the United States. During the time when abortion was banned, Sherri Finkbine ("Miss Sherri") hosted *Romper Room*, a television show for preschoolers. She loved children and planned to have a large family. She had no idea that Arizona's abortion laws would affect her life. Then, in 1962, Finkbine's husband made a trip to Europe. He brought back some Thalidomide, a new tranquilizer that was not available in the United States. Finkbine took some of the drug early in her fifth month of pregnancy.[1] A short time later, she heard reports that Thalidomide caused severe birth defects. In Europe, babies were being born with deformed or missing arms, legs, and ears. Some had paralyzed faces.[2] About half of these babies died a few months after birth.[3] Finkbine's doctor advised her to end her pregnancy. He scheduled her for an abortion at a Phoenix hospital. Finkbine told her story to a reporter. She wanted to warn other women about the dangers of Thalidomide. The story first appeared in a Phoenix newspaper. Then, because Miss Sherri was well known, the story made headlines across the nation. This publicity made people aware that Finkbine's life was not in danger. As a result, the hospital canceled the surgery. Because her life was not in danger, Finkbine could not get a legal abortion in Arizona, or any other state. The Finkbines flew to Sweden for a legal abortion. The embryo was severely deformed.[4]

About seven years later, in 1969, Norma McCorvey was too poor to fly to Sweden for an abortion. The young waitress kept a roof over her head by staying with one friend after another. To make matters worse, she expected to be fired when her boss realized she was pregnant. She already had two children. One lived with McCorvey's mother. The father had custody of the other. McCorvey could not face having another child someone else would raise. She later recalled that time in her life: "I was pregnant with my third child . . . I was . . . a twenty-one-year-old nobody at the end of my rope."[5]

Support for Miss Sherri

According to a poll taken shortly after the incident, 52 percent of Americans supported Sherri Finkbine's abortion whereas 32 percent opposed it.

Source: Laurence H. Tribe, *Abortion: The Clash of Absolutes* (New York: W. W. Norton, 1992), p. 38.

She went to a doctor, seeking an abortion. He told her that because her life was not in danger, she could not get a legal abortion in Texas.

McCorvey filed a suit seeking a legal abortion in March 1970. The courts did not provide a legal solution for her. Her case, however, brought about a change in the law that made abortion legal for other women.

Early Abortion Laws

Early American law was based on the set of rules that people in England lived by and accepted as law. This is called common law. The first settlers brought this law with them to the new land. By common law, abortion performed before quickening (Quickening is the time when the mother first feels the fetus moving inside her.) was not a crime. In 1821, Connecticut became the first state to make abortion after quickening a crime.[6]

At the time these laws were written, midwives and folk doctors (practitioners with no formal medical education) commonly attended women during childbirth. They also provided abortion services. No one, however, including medical doctors, knew much about a woman's body or pregnancy. Women often died from difficult pregnancies and childbirth, as well as abortion.

The American Medical Association

In the mid-1800s, physicians with Doctor of Medicine degrees (MDs) wanted control of medical care in the United States. They formed the American Medical Association (AMA) in 1847. The AMA almost immediately opposed abortion. It claimed that it took this stand to protect women's health. Some, however, believe that the AMA was more interested in forcing midwives and folk doctors out of business. The AMA wanted women to get their health care from medical doctors.

In 1857, Dr. Horatio Storer became an AMA crusader for outlawing abortion.[7] He and other doctors began to speak out about the morality of abortion. In addition, many doctors who studied pregnancy pointed out that the fetus looked human long before the woman felt movement. Many of these doctors felt that abortion was unacceptable long before quickening. As a result, in 1859, the AMA called for a ban on abortion.[8]

Antiabortion Crusade

Throughout the next two decades, Storer and other doctors took their argument to the state capitals. They spoke against abortion on medical, social, and moral grounds.[9] Because of their efforts, one state after another outlawed abortion. By 1899, every state had passed laws to ban abortion. Most states, however, allowed abortion to save the mother's life.[10]

The ban continued well into the twentieth century. Abortions were not done in hospitals. Women, however, still wanted abortions. Some of them found doctors who did safe, illegal abortions in secret. Rich women could travel to Europe for safe abortions. The rest were left in the hands of untrained abortionists. They went to dingy motel rooms or dirty back-alley offices for their abortions. Many of these women bled to death. Some died of infection. Others suffered injuries that would prevent them from ever having children.

Changing Lifestyles

In the mid-1900s, women began changing their attitudes about their role in life. They wanted control over their bodies and their futures. As these women sought jobs, education, and careers, the problems of unwanted pregnancy intensified. Women continued seeking abortions where they could find them. Some went to back-alley abortionists. Others were so desperate they tried to abort themselves. The number of deaths from botched abortions and related infections climbed.

Changing Attitudes

By the early 1960s, attitudes in the medical community began to change. The highly publicized Finkbine story drew attention to the dangers of Thalidomide. Worldwide, an estimated ten thousand to twelve thousand children suffered severe birth defects traced to the drug. It was banned in 1962.[11] A German measles epidemic followed the Thalidomide tragedy. As a result, between 1962 and 1965 another fifteen thousand severely deformed children were born. Some doctors began to think that, at times, birth could be more tragic than abortion.[12] Many of them began to favor making abortion legal in cases where severe birth defects were likely. Other people wanted abortion made legal for other reasons. These reasons included protecting women's health and rights. Thus began a slow trend toward reforming the abortion laws.

California and Colorado soon passed legislation to ease their abortion laws. In 1970, New York, Hawaii, and Alaska legalized abortion.[13] Most states, however, held fast to their strict abortion laws.

Clergy Consultation Service

In 1956, Howard Moody became pastor at Judson Memorial Church in Greenwich Village, New York. While he was the pastor of this church, he developed a compassion for women facing unwanted pregnancy. In 1967, while abortion was illegal, Moody helped found the Clergy Consultation Service. In a short time, about fourteen hundred ministers and rabbis across the country joined Moody's group. This national organization helped women find safe abortion services. Some women were sent outside the United States. Others were put in contact with doctors in states with more liberal abortion laws.[14] During the six years before *Roe* v. *Wade* made abortion legal, the Clergy Consultation Service helped more than one hundred thousand women obtain safe abortions.

Code Name "Jane"

In 1969 a group of Chicago women activists organized The Abortion Counseling Service of Women's Liberation.[15] These women dedicated themselves to helping women find safe abortions. To avoid arrest, they used the code name "Jane." Jane's phone number was passed by word of mouth. At first, members of Jane referred women to doctors who would perform safe abortions. Soon, the demand for abortions exceeded the supply of doctors. To meet this need, the women of Jane learned to do abortions themselves. From 1969 to 1973, some eleven thousand women came to Jane for safe abortions.

Through the 1960s and into the 1970s, many people fought for women's rights, including the right to choose an abortion. When the case that would change the law reached the Supreme Court, it became known as one woman against the district attorney of Dallas County, Texas. *Jane Roe* v. *Wade*, however, would actually bring the abortion issue before the court on behalf of all women.

Chapter 2

Roe v. Wade

When her doctor would not help her get an abortion, Norma McCorvey sought legal advice. The first lawyer she contacted put her in touch with two other sympathetic lawyers. After listening to her story, lawyers Linda Coffee and Sarah Weddington offered to take the case *pro bono*. This means they would not charge a fee. Norma thought they were going to help her get an abortion and accepted the offer.[1] Coffee and Weddington, however, needed a client to name in a case that would challenge the Texas laws against abortion.[2]

Roe v. Wade

Coffee and Weddington filed the suit known as *Roe v. Wade* in the United States District Court for the Northern District of Texas, March 1970.[3] To hide her identity, Norma McCorvey changed her name to "Jane Roe" in the case. Henry Wade was the district attorney of Dallas County, where the suit was filed.

The suit stated that Jane Roe (Norma McCorvey) wanted a legal abortion done by a doctor, under safe conditions. The suit also stated that she was not able to get a legal abortion in Texas because the pregnancy did not threaten her life. In addition, she could not afford to travel to another state for a legal abortion. The suit claimed that the Texas laws were unclear. The laws denied Roe the right of personal privacy guaranteed in the First, Fourth, Fifth, Ninth, and Fourteenth Amendments to the U.S. Constitution. *Roe* v. *Wade* was a class action suit. This means that Jane Roe sued "on behalf of herself and all other women" in a similar situation.[4]

The *Roe* v. *Wade* suit did not seek to punish someone for a criminal act. It did not ask for a reward of money to the plaintiffs (McCorvey and others). The suit asked for a declaratory judgment. This means Jane Roe asked the court to declare the Texas abortion laws unconstitutional. In other words, winning the suit would make abortion legal in Texas. A woman could have an abortion although her life was not in danger. While the case was being decided, Roe asked the court to stop Henry Wade from enforcing the existing abortion law.

▶ Unintended Pregnancies

✓More than 50 percent of pregnancies among American women are unintended; half of these are terminated by abortion.

✓Six out of ten women who have abortions experienced contraceptive failure.

Source: The Alan Guttmacher Institute, New York, 1999, <http://www.agi-usa.org/pubs/fb_induced_abortion.html> (April 20, 2000).

Weddington and Coffee argued the case and won. The decision, however, was not final. Wade immediately filed an appeal with the U.S. Supreme Court. This meant that the case would be argued again. The Supreme Court would either uphold or overturn the decision of the lower court. Meanwhile, District Attorney Wade vowed to prosecute anyone who did an abortion while the case awaited the appeal. At this point, Norma McCorvey was six months' pregnant.[5] She felt she was too far along for a safe abortion. She realized the suit would not solve her problem. Norma later recalled, "It was about me, and maybe all the women who'd come before me, but it was really for all the women who were coming after me."[6] The case reached the U.S. Supreme Court in December 1971. It remained undecided until January 22, 1973. By this time, Norma had given birth to a daughter and put her up for adoption.

The Supreme Court

The Supreme Court is the highest court in the United States. Its rulings determine the law of the land. Nine judges serve on the Supreme Court, a Chief Justice and eight associate justices. After they reach a decision, one justice writes the opinion of the court. Other justices write concurring (agreeing) or dissenting (disagreeing) opinions. The opinions of the Supreme Court are published and made available to every lawyer, judge, and citizen in the nation.

The Decision

In *Roe* v. *Wade*, the Court handed down a 7–2 decision. This means seven justices ruled in favor of the plaintiff, Jane Roe. The Supreme Court found that the Texas abortion law was unclear. It violated the right to personal liberty guaranteed by the U.S. Constitution. The Four-teenth Amendment prohibits the state from depriving "any person of life, liberty, or property without due process of law."[7] Due process is the procedure established by state and fed-eral law that must be followed by the courts and law enforcement agencies to protect individual rights and freedom.

*S*upreme Court Justice Harry A. Blackmun wrote the *Roe* v. *Wade* decision in 1973, which legalized abor-tion in the United States.

Justice Henry A. Blackmun wrote the 1973 opinion of the Court. Justice Blackmun explained that the decision was not easy. The justices were aware "of the sensitive emotional nature of the abortion controversy, [and] of the vigorous opposing views, even among physicians."[8] He went on to write that all one's life experiences including religious training and moral standards are "likely to influence . . . one's thinking and conclusions about abortion."[9]

Before reaching a decision, the justices considered the history of abortion from ancient times to 1973. They read the writings of ancient philosophers and religious leaders. They studied common and statutory law. (Common law is rules for living that are commonly accepted as law.

Statutory law is passed by state or federal legislators.) They also considered the advances in medical knowledge, and changes in society's attitudes. The justices did not try to determine when life begins. It was their duty to examine the Texas law forbidding abortion except to save the life of the mother. And, it was their responsibility to determine whether the state law violated any of the rights guaranteed by the U.S. Constitution. All other states would have to abide by the Supreme Court's decision here.

The Blackmun opinion concluded that "the right to personal privacy includes the abortion decision, but . . . at some point, the state interest as to pro-tection of . . . prenatal life, becomes dominant."[10] This means that the Court recognized a woman's right to choose an abortion until the fetus matured enough to live outside the woman's body. At that point, the Court determined that the state had a responsibility to protect the "prenatal life" (fetus).[11] Thus, the Court divided the nine-month pregnancy into three sections called trimesters. During the first trimester, the Court ruled that a woman had a right to an abortion for any reason. In the second trimester, when abortion becomes more dangerous for the woman, the states may pass laws to protect the woman's health. In the third trimester, when the fetus can live outside the womb, states may pass laws to protect the fetus by prohibiting (forbidding) abortion except to save the life of the mother.[12] This ruling became the law of the land and all states had to revise their laws to uphold the Supreme Court ruling.

Justice Blackmun's opinion clearly allows abortion in the first trimester. Laws regulating abortion in the second and third trimesters were left up to the individual states. In fact, much of the abortion question remains undecided. Some Americans adamantly support a woman's right to abortion. Others, with equal determination, support the unborn's right to life. Few other issues have divided America along such hostile lines.

Chapter 3

What Is Abortion?

By definition, an abortion ends a pregnancy before the time of birth. The embryo or fetus is sometimes expelled naturally. We call this type of abortion a miscarriage. An abortion can also be induced. This means deliberate steps are taken to end the pregnancy. Today, induced abortions are legal, safe, and usually done by doctors.

About 90 percent of abortions are done in the first three months (first trimester) of pregnancy.[1] At this stage, an abortion is relatively simple and poses little risk to the woman. In fact, it is thought to be less dangerous than pregnancy and childbirth, especially for young teens. (Although a young teen may be able to become pregnant, her body may not be ready to meet the demands of pregnancy and childbirth.)

Who Chooses Abortion

Almost half of all pregnancies in America are unplanned. Half of these (about 1.37 million in 1996) are aborted. This means that every year, about 2 percent of American women between the ages of fifteen and forty-four have abortions.[2] These women come from all races and ethnic groups. They represent all income levels and most religious backgrounds. Twenty percent of them are teenagers.[3]

About a million teenagers become pregnant every year. Although 54 percent of these teenagers decide to carry their pregnancies to term, about 40 percent decide to have an abortion.[4] About 6 percent miscarry.

The Abortion Decision

When a woman thinks she may be pregnant, she should have a pregnancy test as soon as possible. She can purchase a pregnancy test kit at a drugstore. Some women's health care and pregnancy centers provide them without charge. If the test is positive, the woman should be examined

Who Has Abortions?

✓ Women age twenty to twenty-four obtain 33 percent of all abortions; teenagers obtain 22 percent.

✓ Two thirds of all abortions are obtained by unmarried women.

✓ About fifteen thousand women have abortions each year because they became pregnant after rape or incest.

Source: S.K. Henshaw and Kathryn Kost, "Abortion Patients in 1994–1995: Characteristics and Contraceptive Use," *Family Planning Perspectives*, vol. 28, 1996, pp. 140–147, 158.

by a doctor to determine how long she has been pregnant. If she wants to become a parent, prenatal care should begin at once. If not, she must make some difficult choices. Talking to someone she trusts will help. She will need the support of close family members or a friend.

Many states require notification of one or both parents before a minor can get an abortion. Some require parental consent.[5] This means that a minor cannot get an abortion unless her parents sign a consent form. Most states that require parental consent also allow judicial bypass. This means the pregnant teen can get a judge to give consent for an abortion.

Counseling

A pregnancy counselor can explain the options, including abortion, parenting, and adoption. Counselors may be found at women's health care organizations. These include Planned Parenthood Federation of America, Inc., and the National Abortion Federation. These organizations are pro-choice. Pro-life organizations offer adoption and parenting counseling only. These include Birthright, Inc., and Crisis Pregnancy Centers. Other helpful counselors may include school nurses, family doctors, and members of the clergy. Other sources may be found in the Yellow Pages under "abortion services" or "adoption." Complete information covering all the options may have to be collected from several places.

Abortion Providers

According to Planned Parenthood Federation of America, Inc., most abortions are done at women's health centers. These centers are clinics that provide health care for women only. Abortions are done in doctor's offices, and some are done in hospitals. The cost varies by location and the stage of pregnancy. According to Planned Parenthood, the cost for an outpatient abortion of a six- to ten-week pregnancy ranges between $300 and $1,700. The cost is higher for more advanced pregnancies. It is also higher when the abortion is done in a hospital.

Two types of abortion can be used to end a pregnancy. Medical abortion ends the pregnancy with drugs. Surgical abortion empties the uterus (womb) with instruments.[6]

Medical Abortion

Medical abortion can be used to end a pregnancy in the first seven weeks. After a pregnancy test, the woman is examined. If the pregnancy is found to be less than seven weeks, one of two drugs can be used to begin the abortion: methotrexate or mifepristone. Methotrexate, approved by the U.S. Food and Drug Administration in 1953 as a cancer drug, can also be used to induce abortion. An injection of methotrexate stops fetal cells from dividing and stops the growth of the embryo. Mifepristone (RU-486), the "abortion pill" widely used in Europe, is now being tested in the United States. The pill blocks the hormone progesterone, which is necessary for the pregnancy to continue. Once either of these drugs takes effect, the pregnancy must end. A few days after taking methotrexate or mifepristone, a second drug, misoprostol is inserted into the vagina. This second drug causes the uterus to contract and expel the pregnancy. A medical abortion can take from three

French Professor Emile-Etienne Beaulieu is the inventor of the abortion drug RU-486. Pro-life groups want to stop the use of this drug in the United States.

days to four weeks. About 5 percent fail and must be followed with a surgical abortion.[7]

First-Trimester Surgical Abortion

The most common method of ending a pregnancy in the first trimester is suction aspiration. A local anesthetic is usually used to numb the cervix (the muscular neck of the uterus). The opening in the cervix is then enlarged (dilated). This allows the insertion of a tube attached to a suction machine. The suction pulls the contents of the uterus through the tube and into a collection bottle. The pregnancy ends. A spoon-shaped instrument, called a curette, may be used to remove any remaining tissue from the uterus. This procedure takes five to ten minutes. During the next few days the woman will have vaginal bleeding similar to her menstrual period. As with any surgery, there is some risk. The most common is infection. Sometimes the uterus is damaged.[8]

Second-Trimester Surgical Abortion

About 10 percent of abortions performed in the United States are done in the second trimester.[9] Many of these are performed for medical reasons. For example, a woman might develop a severe heart problem or a disease such as diabetes. This could put her life at risk if she continues the pregnancy. Others, however, result from young, unmarried women who refuse to accept their condition. They wait and hope the problem will go away. By the time they realize it is not going away, they are into the second trimester. Others have irregular periods and do not realize they are pregnant in the early months. Some have to save or raise money for an abortion. When a woman waits to make her decision, a more difficult procedure may be required.

In the second trimester, the cervix must be further enlarged. Suction will not completely empty the uterus, and surgical forceps (an instrument that grips and holds) must be used to remove the fetus. Any remaining tissue is scraped from the uterine walls with a curette. This procedure takes ten to thirty minutes. "Dilation and evacuation" is performed under general anesthesia (the woman is put to sleep). It poses a greater risk of heavy bleeding and infection.[10]

Another method, sometimes used later in the second trimester, is the induction or instillation method. This method is done in the hospital under local anesthesia. The doctor injects a medication (prostaglandin, urea, or saline solution) directly into the uterus through the abdomen. The fetus dies. Uterine contractions begin within a few hours and the fetus is expelled some time later.[11]

The Third Trimester

Abortion is rare after the twenty-third week of pregnancy.[12] Today, most complications of pregnancy can be found, and treated, in the first and second trimesters. When difficulties arise that threaten the mother's life in the third trimester, labor can be induced. By this time, a living premature infant can be delivered. Four out of ten premature babies born in the twenty-fourth to twenty-sixth week of pregnancy survive.[13] To do so, they need intensive care in a modern neonatal unit, available in most large hospitals. After the twenty-sixth week

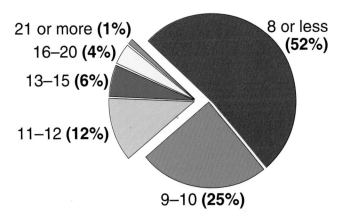

When Women Have Abortions

(in weeks)

21 or more **(1%)**
16–20 **(4%)**
13–15 **(6%)**
11–12 **(12%)**
9–10 **(25%)**
8 or less **(52%)**

Eighty-nine Percent of Abortions Occur in the First Twelve Weeks of Pregnancy.

Source: The Alan Guttmacher Institute, New York, 1999, <http://www.agi-usa.org/pubs/fb_abortion2/fb_abort2.html> (April 20, 2000).

of pregnancy, most premature babies survive. Born before they have fully developed, however, some have lifelong health problems.

The Choice

Today, abortions performed in the first trimester are relatively simple, with little risk. Less than one percent of all abortions result in major complications. These include serious pelvic infection or extensive bleeding that requires further surgery or a blood transfusion. Statistics from 1998 show that one death occurs in every one hundred fifty thousand legal abortions. More than four times as many women died from illegal abortions before *Roe v. Wade*.[14] Unwanted pregnancy, however, is still a crisis. Deciding what to do cannot wait very long. At some point the choice, no matter what it is, cannot be changed. Therefore, a woman must consider all her options in a limited period of time. She must be willing to accept her decision, whatever it is, and live with it.

Chapter 4

The Conflict

The *Roe* v. *Wade* decision was not unanimous. In a divided vote, seven justices voted in favor of Roe. Two justices, Byron Raymond White and William Hobbs Rehnquist, voted in favor of Wade. White and Rehnquist wrote the dissenting opinions. This means they wrote papers explaining their votes.

Justice White wrote that the Court decision valued "the convenience of the pregnant mother more than the life or potential life she carries."[1] He opposed this view. He also opposed the overturning of the Texas law.

Justice Rehnquist did not agree that the Fourth Amendment privacy rights include abortion. According to Rehnquist, the privacy the Court found here was not "even a distant relative of the freedom from searches and seizures protected by the Fourth Amendment."[2]

Some Americans agree with the Court's *Roe* v. *Wade* decision. Others agree with Justices White and Rehnquist. Some join organized pro-choice and pro-life groups. (The pro-choice groups support a woman's right to choose abortion, whereas the pro-life groups oppose abortion under most circumstances.) Others simply have an opinion. People argue over whose rights come first—the woman's or the fetus's. They question the morality on both sides of the issue. They debate over when life begins.

We might settle some of the abortion conflict if the question of when life begins could be answered. Some say life begins at conception; others say forty days later. Still others say at birth, with the first breath.

When Does Life Begin?

The Texas attorney representing Wade argued that "Life begins at conception and is present throughout pregnancy."[3] The Supreme Court, however, refused to consider the question of when human life begins. Justice Blackmun wrote: "When those trained in . . . medicine, philosophy, and theology are unable to [answer], the Judiciary . . . is not in a position to . . . answer."[4]

Little was known about the development of the fetus in the early 1970s. Activity inside the womb remained a secret until the invention of modern imaging equipment. Today, however, doctors and researchers can see inside the womb. With ultrasound, they can view an embryo as early as five weeks from the woman's last menstrual period.[5] A few weeks later, they can watch the image of a moving fetus on a television screen. For many years now, they have studied the fetus in the womb.

Conception (fertilizing of the egg) usually takes place about fourteen days after the woman's last menstrual period. In the next few days, the fertilized egg attaches itself to the wall of the uterus and

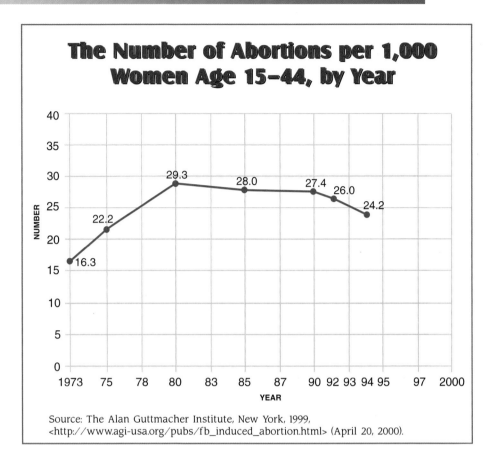

The Number of Abortions per 1,000 Women Age 15–44, by Year

Source: The Alan Guttmacher Institute, New York, 1999, <http://www.agi-usa.org/pubs/fb_induced_abortion.html> (April 20, 2000).

begins to grow. As it develops, the fertilized egg becomes an embryo and then a fetus. This is determined by the length of the pregnancy. A fetus delivered after the twenty-fourth week of pregnancy can survive outside the womb.[6]

Whose Rights?

Even if everyone were to agree that life begins at a certain time, the conflict would continue over whose rights count the most.

Those on the pro-choice side of the issue focus on the woman's rights. They believe that every woman has the right to decide whether she will have children, and when and how many she will have. They also believe that every child has the right to be wanted and loved. In their view, legal abortion protects these rights when an unwanted pregnancy occurs. Although abortion has been legal since 1973, they see the pro-life movement as a threat. They worry that the Court might someday overturn the *Roe* v. *Wade* decision. This could happen if another case came before a more conservative Supreme Court.

Pro-life supporters believe that the life of the unborn child is no less valuable than that of the mother. They think women should take responsibility for their actions. First, a woman should not conceive if she does not want a child. Second, she should be prepared to deal with the consequences of her actions. This would include carrying the pregnancy to term, and parenting the child or placing him or her for adoption. She should do this at her own emotional and financial expense. In the pro-life view, an abortion ends the life of an unborn child. Some believe abortion is murder.

The Religious Debate

Abortion is one conflict, among many, that divides the religious community.

Among Christians, the Catholic, Southern Baptist, and Mormon churches officially oppose abortion.[7] Some people within these churches, however, believe that a woman should have the right to choose abortion. Many of those who disagree with their church's stand have formed organizations to support pro-choice. These organizations include Catholics for a Free Choice and the Religious Coalition for Reproductive Choice.

*A*ttorney Sarah Weddington, left, was the keynote speaker at a lunch that honored the twenty-fifth anniversary of the *Roe* v. *Wade* decision. Weddington, who argued the landmark case, represented Norma McCorvey.

The members of The Religious Coalition for Reproductive Choice include some thirty-five Christian and Jewish organizations.

Other people who want their church to support choice have worked to change their denomination's doctrine (official beliefs). For example, the Southern Baptists (the largest Protestant church in America) ended a twelve-year dispute over doctrine in 1991. Neither side won. The church divided into two branches.[8] The Southern Baptist Convention (SBC) still opposes abortion. The newly formed Cooperative Baptist Fellowship (CBF) is pro-choice.

Other denominations, including the Presbyterian

Church in the United States and United Methodists, are pro-choice. They have experienced similar struggles with members who are pro-life.

The abortion issue is less controversial among Jews. The Reform, Conservative, and Reconstructionist movements consider abortion a personal matter. The Orthodox Jews, however, allow abortion only to protect the health and life of the mother.

Basic Islamic doctrine does not forbid abortion. Within fundamentalist Moslem countries, however, abortion is illegal except to save the life of the mother.[9]

The three major religions of the world, Christianity, Judaism, and Islam include the books of the Old Testament in the sacred literature. These scriptures, however, are silent on abortion. Still, religious people draw support for their beliefs from these texts.

The Medical Community

The abortion conflict brought about changes in the oath medical students take when they become doctors. The wording of the oath varies from school to school. The original oath is named after the ancient Greek physician Hippocrates. The Hippocratic Oath has been the basis for medical ethics in the world for at least two thousand five hundred years.[10]

Revising the oath has been necessary to reflect advances in medical knowledge, changing attitudes, political correctness, and the law. For example, the ancient Hippocratic Oath (translated from classic Greek) contained the phrase, "I will not give to a woman an abortive remedy."[11] In other words, doctors pledged that they would not perform abortions.

Graduating medical students at Johns Hopkins University recited the original oath at graduation ceremonies in 1968. This triggered a protest. As a result, the university adopted a new version of the oath, without the reference to abortion. Many other medical schools took similar action.

Medical students, however, represent a wide range of views. Some oppose abortion and prefer the wording of the original oath. In 1999, more than thirty University of Oklahoma medical students requested a separate graduation ceremony. They wanted their oath of ethics to include the original antiabortion phrase.[12]

The abortion conflict affects doctors when they begin practice. Sometimes it is the reason they end their medical careers. In recent years, many doctors who once did abortions no longer do them. Some have changed their position on abortion. Violence at women's clinics has driven others from the practice. According to Planned Parenthood, most doctors who no longer provide abortion services have done so out of fear for their lives.

Political Conflict

Abortion is a hot political issue. The Democrats are fairly united in their support of choice. For many years, the Republican party has officially opposed abortion. A growing number of party members, however, support choice. Before the 2000 presidential election, some Republicans began softening their stance.[13] This means they were willing to allow choice because it is legal. Many of them, however, continue to oppose abortion personally.[14] In addition, some pro-life Republican candidates no longer seek a constitutional amendment banning all abortions. They believe these changes in politics are necessary to win a future national election. Still, some fear the new position will hurt them in the primaries. As a result, some candidates try to avoid the issue altogether. Others, who feel more confident in their stand, continually bring it up.

The abortion issue touches almost every American citizen in some way. Some will consider the issue in deciding how they will cast their vote. Others will face the issue in a personal way. They are the ones who will face the choice.

Chapter 5

The Pro-Choice Camp

The birth control pill became available in the early 1960s. This, and the *Roe* v. *Wade* decision in 1973, gave women greater control over their reproductive lives. The pill sometimes failed.

With legal and safe abortion, however, women could still avoid or delay motherhood. Unplanned pregnancy no longer posed a threat to education or career plans. Still, the issue was not so easily settled. Advances in medical technology soon brought new legal and moral concerns about abortion. Many women bristled at the threat to their newly gained freedom.

The Pro-Choice Movement

Pro-choice supporters come from all walks of life. The activists work hard to promote pro-choice issues. They lobby Congress, make speeches, and work at pro-choice organizations. Many men and women who want to help protect a woman's right to choose abortion officially join groups such as the National Organization of Women. Some devote time

Reasons for Choosing Abortion

Planned Parenthood lists several reasons a woman might give for deciding to have an abortion:

✓ She is not ready for the way becoming a parent will change her life. It would be hard to keep her job, continue her education, and/or care for her other children.

✓ She cannot afford a baby now.

✓ She does not want to be a single parent; she does not want to marry her partner; he cannot or will not marry her; or she is not in a relationship.

✓ She is not ready for the responsibility.

✓ She does not want anyone to know that she has had sex or is pregnant.

✓ She is too young or too immature to have a child.

✓ She has all the children she wants.

✓ Her husband, partner, or parent wants her to have an abortion.

✓ She or the fetus has a health problem.

✓ She was a victim of rape or incest.

Source: "Abortion: Commonly Asked Questions," Planned Parenthood, <http://www.plannedparenthood.org/abortion/abortquestions.html# whydowomen> (April 20, 2000).

and energy to an organization. Others donate money to support the cause. Some people who are pro-choice do not join an organization.

Pro-choice supporters believe everyone should decide when and if parenthood fits into his or her life. They believe that women should not be forced to sacrifice education, careers, or other plans to carry an unwanted pregnancy to term. They believe that women who become pregnant from rape or incest should not be forced to continue the pregnancy. They also believe a woman has the right to choose abortion to protect her health and her future. This includes refusing to carry a badly deformed fetus to term. They see abortion as a protection for women's rights.[1]

A Woman's Right

The main argument from the pro-choice supporters is that a woman's body belongs to her. She has the right to control it. To most women, this means deciding when motherhood fits into her life. It includes choosing whose children she will bear, how many she will have, and when.

Pro-choicers note that a woman and a man create a pregnancy. They point out that consequences of unplanned pregnancy often fall solely on the woman. In their view, women should not be victims of their gender, forced into motherhood before they are ready. They see unplanned pregnancy as a threat to equality in the workplace and to a woman's future, health, and well-being.

The Fetus

Pro-choicers reject the idea that the fertilized egg, embryo, or fetus has the same status as a child.

They argue that granting it rights equal or superior to those of a woman "serves to diminish women."[2]

Pro-choice activists do not call the fetus a baby. Instead, they include it with the pregnancy that is removed during an abortion. This includes the fetus, amniotic sac, lining of the uterus, and placenta. They use nonperson terms such as "contents of the uterus" and "product of conception." Their aim is to keep the focus on the woman, her rights, and her well-being.

Religion and Choice

Many people mistakenly believe that the abortion debate is between the religious and not religious. Some think that all religious people are pro-life and against abortion. Before the *Roe* v. *Wade* decision, however, pastors of various churches across America helped many women find safe abortions. In 1973, about the time *Roe* v. *Wade* became law, several religious groups formed the Religious Coalition for Abortion Rights. Today, the organization is known as the Religious Coalition for Reproductive Choice. Forty national ecumenical Christian, Jewish, and other religious groups have joined this coalition. (Ecumenical churches tolerate other beliefs besides their own.) Members of the coalition support the idea that the abortion decision can be moral, ethical, and religiously acceptable.[3] They want women to be free to decide when to have children, based on their own beliefs.

The Political Arena

Pro-choice activists work to get pro-choice supporters elected to office at the local, state, and federal level. Republicans gained control of the House of

Representatives and Senate in the election of 1994. By 1998, only 131 of the 435 members of the House were pro-choice, and only 33 of the 100 senators were.[4] In recent years, state governments have also moved toward the pro-life side. As a result, fifty-five bills to restrict abortion passed at the state level in 1997. These restrictions include waiting periods and parental consent or notification. In other words, in some states women must wait twenty-four to forty-eight hours after deciding to have an abortion. According to some state laws, minors must contact their parents before getting an abortion. Pro-choice supporters argue that these restrictions make obtaining an abortion more difficult. In addition, the resulting delays put women at greater risk from later abortions. They would like to make the abortion laws the same in every state. Then, some women would not have to go to another state for an abortion. This would reduce the cost and emotional stress for many women facing an unwanted pregnancy.

Parental Consent

Pro-choice supporters view parental consent laws as an attempt to make abortion more difficult for young women. They argue that if a woman is old enough to be forced into motherhood, she is old enough to make the abortion decision. They point out that requiring parental consent often delays the abortion decision. As a result, an abortion may pose more risk to the pregnant teen. Statistics say that 45 percent of pregnant teens tell their parents. In fact, most parents support their daughter's decision to have an abortion.[5] Teens who do not tell their parents have reasons for not doing so. Some do not want their parents to know they have had sex. Others fear they would be forced to bear the child against their will. Still others are afraid their parents will react violently to the news. Most states have provided a judicial bypass for teens who can not tell their parents. This means a judge can grant permission for the abortion.

In 1998, twenty-two states had parental consent laws.[6] Pro-choicers condemn these laws for violating a woman's right to privacy and restricting her constitutional right to abortion.

Education

Pro-choicers consider education a high priority. They work to make women aware of their rights. They also promote sex education in schools. This includes contraception (birth control) information. They believe that making contraception available to

TEENS AND ABORTION

✓Nearly four out of every ten teen pregnancies end in abortion.

✓Sixty-one percent of minors who have abortions do so with at least one parent's knowledge. The majority of parents support their daughter's decision to have an abortion.

Sources: U.S Teenage Pregnancy Statistics, 1999, *Sex and America's Teenagers*, The Alan Guttmacher Institute, <http://www.agi-usa.org/pubs/fb_abortion2/fb_teen_sex.html> (April 20, 2000).

male and female teenagers will decrease unwanted pregnancy and abortion.

Violence

The abortion issue stirs emotions to the boiling point on both sides. Some people in the pro-life camp have become radical and out of control. Between 1977 and 1983, these extremists bombed eight clinics and burned thirteen more. The National Abortion Federation counted 149 acts of violence during these years.[7] These acts included bombings, arson, vandalism, and death threats.

Some antiabortion extremists took these actions to prevent women from getting abortions. They also motivated others to join them in protests that blocked the entrances to an abortion clinic in 1987. In 1991, the hatred flared, adding two attempted murders to the list of violent acts. Then, in March 1993, shots rang out and Dr. David Gunn fell dead outside a clinic in Pensacola, Florida. Other shootings followed.

The federal government took steps to protect women's right to abortion. In May 1994, President Clinton signed the Freedom of Access to Clinic Entrances Act. This act forbids the use of "force or threat of force . . . to intimidate . . . any persons from obtaining or providing reproductive health services."[8]

Still, the violence continues. In January 1998, a bomb exploded at a women's health clinic in Birmingham, Alabama, killing a police officer and critically injuring a nurse.[9] In October of the same year, Dr. Bernard Slepian was killed by a sniper's bullet in his own home in East Amherst, New York.

These are criminal acts. Several of these cases

have been solved. The criminals have been convicted and are serving their sentences. Others are still under investigation.

The battle did not end with *Roe* v. *Wade*. Abortion rights are being altered as states add new restrictions. Pro-choice activists still fight state laws. They fear that one day a new case will come before a conservative Supreme Court and *Roe* v. *Wade* will be overturned. In addition, women and doctors are intimidated by the threat of violence at the clinics. Pro-choice activists sometimes must escort women in and out of the clinics.

Pro-life groups do not condone the use of

*D*r. Barnett Slepian, who performed legal abortions, was killed in his home by a sniper's bullet on October 23, 1998. Here, two agents from the Department of Alcohol, Tobacco, and Firearms investigate the crime scene.

violence. The National Right to Life Committee (NRLC), the largest pro-life group in the United States, has more than three thousand local chapters across the nation. It condemns "any acts of violence used by individuals regardless of their motivation . . . Violence plays no part in the work of the pro-life movement."

Chapter 6

The Pro-Life Camp

Americans have disagreed about abortion for more than one hundred fifty years. Those who were opposed to abortion won in the mid-1800s when abortion was banned. Those in favor of abortion won in 1973 when abortion was made legal.

The pro-life activists, as we know them today, began to organize shortly after the first abortion clinics opened in the 1970s. Some young Catholics decided to protest against abortion. They modeled their protests after the civil rights sit-ins of the 1960s.[1] A few Protestants joined them in the first sit-ins in 1975. The activists sat down in the doorways of clinics, blocking the entrance. They refused to move, sometimes joining hands to pray. They were frequently arrested and considered risking jail part of the protest.

People from all walks of life and all faiths joined the pro-life movement. Some of them took their stand against abortion by opening pregnancy-care centers. These centers offer help to pregnant

A person dressed as the Grim Reaper joined a demonstration of antiabortion and pro-choice activists in Buffalo, New York, on April 20, 1999. The opposing groups confronted each other in front of a women's health clinic.

women who choose to carry their pregnancies to term. They provide food, shelter, clothing, and medical care.[2]

The Pro-Life Movement

Catholics and Evangelical Christians make up a majority of pro-life activists.[3] (Evangelicals do not accept any other beliefs but their own.[4]) These people are likely to favor the traditional family. This means the wife/mother works in the home while the husband/father provides the family income. Most pro-lifers view motherhood and child care as an important and fulfilling role for women. They promote abstinence from sexual intercourse except between husband and wife. They believe a woman facing an unwanted pregnancy should carry the child to term and make the best of her situation. They use less technical, more emotional terms. To them a fetus is a baby or unborn child. The pregnant woman is a mother. Pro-lifers do not agree that a woman's right to control her body includes the right to have an abortion. They believe the unborn child has a right to life.

Some people who want to support the pro-life position join organizations such as the National Right to Life Committee (NRLC). NRLC helps women facing unwanted pregnancy avoid abortion. This includes helping them obtain medical care, financial support, and adoption services. The organization is also a political action group. This means it works to get pro-life candidates elected. It also tries to influence legislation favorable to the pro-life position. NRLC has state branches and offices located throughout the United States.

It's a Baby!

Pro-lifers believe that human life begins at conception. This means they believe life begins as soon as the egg and sperm unite. They believe that a woman has a baby in her womb from the first day of pregnancy. In their view, to destroy that life is to destroy a child. They want every woman who is considering abortion to be aware of fetal development. They want her to know how the fetus she is carrying looks at the time she is considering abortion. Some pregnancy centers have ultrasound equipment. They let the woman see the developing fetus in her womb.

Education

Pro-lifers believe education is necessary to stop abortion. They argue that if women knew more about fetal development, they would not have abortions.

They want people to know that the heart of the fetus begins to beat about twenty-one days after conception.[5] This is about the time the woman notices she has missed her first period. Doctors can detected the embryo's brain waves about the time the woman misses her second period.[6] At eight weeks, the embryo officially becomes a fetus. While still in the first trimester, the fetus sleeps and wakes. It hiccups. It flexes its arms and legs.[7] Pro-life people think that a woman who is considering abortion should know these facts.

The Catholics and Fundamentalist Christians in the pro-life movement strongly object to sex education in school. They fight the distribution of birth control information on the grounds that it may encourage teen sexual activity. They argue that sex education is the parents' responsibility.

Sometimes pro-life demonstrators carry large pictures of aborted fetuses. Many people find these pictures very offensive. Pro-lifers argue that the truth should not be ignored.

Health Threat

Pro-lifers argue that abortion is harmful to a woman's health. They cite examples of injuries to the cervix and uterus that may cause miscarriage in later pregnancies. They contend that abortion procedures are painful for the woman and torture for the unborn child. They claim that ultrasound images of the fetus during abortion reveal that it reacts to the pain. Furthermore, during second-trimester abortions with saline injections, the mother feels the fetus move about inside her as it dies. Pro-lifers argue that such experiences can leave a woman emotionally scarred.

Change of Heart

Some pro-choice activists, abortion-clinic workers, and doctors are haunted by the victims of abortion. Many of these people have changed their views. One of these is Norma McCorvey, Jane Roe in *Roe* v. *Wade*. McCorvey was strongly pro-choice until 1994. After meeting Flip Benham, the director of Operation Rescue, she was overcome by feelings of guilt. She later recalled realizing that she "might have been responsible for the deaths of 35 million children."[8] McCorvey immediately quit her job at an abortion clinic in Dallas. She then joined Roe No More Ministries, a pro-life organization that offers crisis pregnancy counseling and alternatives to abortion.

Political Action

Pro-life activists support political candidates who favor their position. They work hard to get legislation passed to restrict abortion. In this way, they hope to chisel away at legalized abortion until they get it banned again.

Pro-lifers see laws that require waiting periods and parental consent as steps toward reducing the number of abortions. They think that a woman who has decided to have an abortion might change her mind during the waiting period. They hope that involving parents in a teen's decision will give her the option of keeping her baby.

*N*orma McCorvey, who was Jane Roe in the landmark *Roe* v. *Wade* case, is shown attending church services in Dallas in 1998. McCorvey was a pro-choice activist until 1995, when she changed her views and joined the pro-life cause.

The abortion issue brings feelings of distress and sadness to people on both sides of the issue. Many scientists support the pro-life position that the fetus is a baby. According to the highest court in the land, however, abortion is a woman's right. Some opinion polls indicate that most Americans believe abortion is morally wrong.[9] They also show that over 60 percent of those polled agree that women should have the right to have an abortion.[10] This means many Americans have mixed feelings. They care about the woman facing the unwanted pregnancy. They also care about her unborn child. They feel pro-choice when they think about the woman. They feel pro-life when they think about the fetus.[11]

Chapter 7

Other Choices

A woman facing an unwanted pregnancy needs understanding. She also needs the answers to many questions, some she may not think to ask. Unfortunately, the answers a woman gets may depend on the personal view of the person she asks. Many people have strong opinions about abortion. Some people who claim to be unbiased, are very biased. According to Margaret Carlson of *Time* magazine, "We all lie, to ourselves and one another . . . lest we give one inch in a war over abortion that rages on."[1] As a result, obtaining all the necessary information may require many sources.

To make the right choice, the woman must know the truth about her options. She has two choices besides abortion: She can carry her baby to term and raise it, or she can carry the baby to term and place it for adoption.

Raising the Baby

Many women decide to carry their unintended pregnancies to term. In fact, about 54 percent of pregnant teens give birth.[2] A teen mother will need financial and emotional support. She will also need childcare so she can complete her education. Her family is the best source for this help.

Many women do not have supportive families. They can still find the help that will allow them to keep their babies. Many pro-life organizations see helping women through "crisis pregnancies" as the best way to stop abortion. Two of these are Birthright, Inc., and Crisis Pregnancy Centers. They offer free pregnancy testing and counseling. They discourage abortion. They provide most of a pregnant woman's needs, including medical, legal, educational, and housing assistance. They offer childbirth classes, maternity clothes, and layettes. These organizations either provide the services themselves or refer the woman to other agencies. Their help, however, usually ends soon after the

Teen Sex and Pregnancy
Teen Sex and Pregnancy

Teen Sex and Pregnancy

✓A sexually active teen who does not use contraception has a 90 percent chance of becoming pregnant within one year.

✓Each year, almost one million teenage women become pregnant.

✓Seventy-eight percent of teen pregnancies are unplanned, making up about one fourth of all accidental pregnancies annually.

Source: *Teen Sex & Pregnancy*, The Alan Guttmacher Institute, 1999, <http://www.agi-usa.org/pubs/fb_teen_sex.html> (April 20, 2000).

child is born. An uneducated teen facing eighteen years of parenthood may become dependent on welfare, with little hope of ever rising above the poverty level. Almost 4 million American mothers received welfare in 1993. Fifty-five percent of these women gave birth in their teens.[3]

Adoption

Raising a baby as a poor, single parent is hard. Adoption may be a better choice. The organizations mentioned earlier will help a woman carry her pregnancy to term and place the baby for adoption. Once she decides to place her baby for adoption, they will help her contact an adoption agency. The adoption arrangements are usually made before the child is born. Placing a child for adoption is a very caring and loving act. After the woman has given birth, these organizations will help her put her life back in order and continue her education or find a job.

The Hard Choices

Hard choices accompany unintended pregnancy. The decision to have an abortion means ending the life of the fetus. The decision to place a baby for adoption means giving birth only to leave the hospital alone. Since most women who face unwanted pregnancies are single, most who choose to raise their child will be single parents. Babies and children are demanding. They put a strain on two parents. These same demands on one parent can be overwhelming. Preventing unintended pregnancy is the ideal solution.

The Best Choice

Using birth control reduces the risk of unintended pregnancy. However, it may give unmarried teens a false sense of security. No contraceptive method is 100 percent effective. In the mid-1990s, 60 percent of woman who had abortions became pregnant because their birth control method failed.[4]

Although teenagers may think that abstinence (no sex) is too difficult and unfair, the risks that accompany premarital (before marriage) sex are extremely unfair to women. The man can walk away, and many do. It is the woman who gets pregnant and must face the tough choices. The best choice for every woman, from puberty on, is to avoid the possibility of unwanted pregnancy.

Common Ground

Most Americans have an opinion about abortion. Some cannot ignore the plight of the woman facing unwanted pregnancy. Others mourn the death of the unborn child. Many struggle and are unable to decide the abortion issue for themselves. They abhor the violent attacks on abortion clinics and against the doctors who perform the legal operations. This abortion conflict has raged for more than twenty-five years. While some people continue the battle, others seek solutions to the problem.

In 1992, some strongly committed pro-lifers and pro-choicers joined forces to form the Common Ground Network for Life and Choice.[5] The Buffalo, New York, based network has now expanded, with branches in Cleveland; Denver; Dallas; Washington, D.C.; and other areas.[6] No one is asked to give up his or her basic beliefs. Instead, the members work together to find shared concerns. These include

*P*ro-choice supporters gather on the steps of the Supreme Court in Washington, D.C. Although abortion is currently legal, many supporters worry that if a conservative Supreme Court is appointed, it would overturn the *Roe* v. *Wade* decision.

preventing teen pregnancy, promoting adoption, providing adequate day care, and many other women's issues. In seeking common ground, the organization's members hope to shift the focus from the conflict to helping women. Jan Parshall, a pro-life activist, says, "I think this debate would be softened to a whisper if we could go back and eliminate the causes (that lead women to choose abortion)."[7] Pro-choicer Maggi Cage adds, "A battleground mentality does nothing for either side. The person who loses out is the woman [who is] trying to make a decision about whether or not to terminate a pregnancy."[8]

Meeting in small discussion groups, the

Common Ground Network is taking the abortion issue out of the political and legal arena as it confronts the problems of real people. In St. Louis, local members helped a young pregnant girl keep her baby. A pro-choice member donated prenatal care, and pro-life volunteers provided transportation to her doctor appointments.[9]

Instead of taking a stand for or against abortion, many Americans are taking a stand against the causes of abortion. Some organizations encourage teens (boys and girls) to commit to abstinence. Others make it easier for women to keep their babies. Others fight for affordable child care. The focus on the common areas of concern seems to be helping to some extent. In the 1990s, the number of abortions decreased.

Still, the controversy rages on. The pro-choice side is determined to keep abortion legal. The pro-life side is working to make it illegal again. They hope to bring the abortion issue before a conservative Supreme Court someday. This would change the law. It would not end the conflict.

Pro-Choice Hotlines:
The National Abortion Federation
1436 U Street NW, Ste. 103
Washington, D.C., 20009
(800) 772-9100
in Canada: (800) 424-2280
<http://www.prochoice.org/pregnant/hotline.htm>

Planned Parenthood Federation of America
810 Seventh Avenue
New York, NY 10019
(800) 230-PLAN

Pro-Life Hotlines:
Birthright USA
(800) 550-4900
<http://www.birthright.org>

Crisis Pregnancy Centers
(Crisis Pregnancy Centers have telephone numbers for
each state. Look in your phone book or go online to
find a local telephone number for your area.)
<http://www.pregnancycenters.org>

Internet:
Full Text of Supreme Court Cases
<http://www.tourolaw.edu/patch/SupremeCourtCases.
html> See Roe *v.* Wade.

The Allen Guttmacher Institute
<http://www.agi-usa.org>

For More Information

Chapter 1. When Abortion Was Banned

1. Laurence H. Tribe, *Abortion: A Clash of Absolutes* (New York: W. W. Norton & Company, 1990), p. 37.

2. Roger Rosenblatt, *Life Itself: Abortion in the American Mind* (New York: Random House, 1992), p. 90.

3. (Staff-written from wire reports), "Thalidomide: A History," *The (North Carolina) News & Observer*, May 22, 1997.

4. Tribe, p. 37.

5. Norma McCorvey with Andy Meisler, *I Am Roe: My Life,* Roe *v.* Wade, *and Freedom of Choice* (New York: HarperCollins, 1994), p. 101.

6. *Roe* v. *Wade,* 410 U.S. 113, January 22, 1973.

7. Eric Foner and John A. Garraty, eds., "Abortion," *The Reader's Companion to American History*, (New York: Houghton Mifflin Company), electric library download.

8. Tribe, p. 30.

9. Foner and Garraty.

10. Carl N. Flanders, *Library in a Book: Abortion* (New York: Facts on File, 1991), p. 6.

11. "Thalidomide: A History."

12. Tribe, p. 37.

13. Leslie J. Reagan, *When Abortion Was a Crime: Women, Medicine, and the Law in the United States, 1967–1977* (Berkeley, Calif.: University of California Press), p. 241.

14. Carole E. Joffe, *Doctors of Conscience: The Struggle to Provide Abortion Before and After* Roe *v.* Wade (Boston: Beacon Press, 1995), p. 10.

15. Laura Kaplan, *The Story of Jane* (New York: Pantheon Books, 1995), pp. ix–x.

Chapter 2. *Roe v. Wade*

1. Norma McCorvey with Andy Meisler, *I am Roe: My Life,* Roe *v.* Wade, *and Freedom of Choice* (New York: HarperCollins, 1994), p. 123.

2. Ibid., p. 113.

3. *Roe* v. *Wade*, 410 U.S. 113, January 22, 1973.

4. Ibid.

5. Norma McCorvey with Andy Meisler, p. 126.

6. Ibid., p. 127.

7. Fourteenth Amendment to the U.S. Constitution.

8. *Roe* v. *Wade*.

9. Ibid.

10. Ibid.

11. Ibid.

12. Ibid.

Chapter 3.   What is Abortion?

1. Susan Dudley, "Women Who Have Abortions," *National Abortion Federation*, 1995, <http://www.prochoice.org> (March 13, 1998).

2. "Facts in Brief: Induced Abortion," *The Alan Guttmacher Institute*, 1998, <http://www.agi-usa.org> (March 20, 1998).

3. Ibid.

4. Ibid.

5. Pat Donovan, "Special Analysis—Teen to Consent to Reproductive Health Care Commonly Recognized at State Level," *Contemporary Women's Issues Database*, vol. 8, September 1, 1997, pp. 3ff.

6. "What is Medical Abortion?," *The National Abortion Federation*, 1997, <http://www.prochoice.org> (March 13, 1998).

7. Ibid.

8. "Fact Sheet: What is a Surgical Abortion?," *The National Abortion Federation*, 1995, <http://www.prochoice.org> (March 13, 1998).

9. Dudley.

10. "Fact Sheet: What is a Surgical Abortion?"

11. Ibid.

12. Dudley.

13. "Fetal Development," (According to the Ohio Department of Health), *Ohio Right to Life*, September 1995.

14. "Facts in Brief: Induced Abortion."

Chapter 4. The Conflict

1. Justice White, *Roe* v. *Wade: Dissent #2*, January 1973.

2. Justice Rehnquist, *Roe* v. *Wade: Dissent #1*, January 22, 1973.

3. Ibid.

4. Justice Blackmun, Opinion of the Court, *Roe* v. *Wade*, 410 U.S. 113.

5. Lennart Nilsson, *A Child is Born* (New York: Dell Publishing, 1990), p. 82.

6. Ibid., pp. 82, 177.

7. Jeffrey L. Sheler, "The Theology of Abortion," *U.S. News & World Report*, March 3, 1992, pp. 54–55.

8. "SBC or CBF? Make an Informed Decision," *The Conservative Record*, May 1999, <http://www.ncbaptist.com/May99/CBF.htm> (October 29,1999).

9. Ellen Hale, "Our Crowded Planet: a Woman's Burden—Abortion Old as Man, Controversy is Recent," *Gannett News Service*, September 5, 1994, electronic library download.

10. Stephen Spruiell, "U. Oklahoma Med Students Disagree With Oath," *University Wire*, May 26, 1999.

11. Joyce Price, "Hippocratic Oath Undergoes Politically Correct Surgery: Revisions More 'Self-centered' Than Patient Centered," *The Washington Times*, June 2, 1996, p. 8.

12. Spruiell.

13. Richard L. Berke, *The New York Times*, "GOP Wary of Blasting Abortion Candidates' Words Careful," *Arizona Republic*, June 21, 1999, p. A1.

14. Ibid.

Chapter 5. The Pro-Choice Camp

1. Faye D. Ginsburg, *Contested Lives: The Abortion Debate in the American Community* (Berkeley/Los Angeles/London: University of California Press, 1989), p. 7.

2. "Nine Reasons Why Abortions are Legal," *Planned Parenthood*, March 1989.

3. "General Information," Religious Coalition for Reproductive Choice, n.d., <http://www.rcrc.org/rcrc/geninfo.html> (March 24, 1998).

4. "Abortion and the Republicans: Idealists v. Realists," *The Economist*, vol. 346, January 24, 1998.

5. "Facts in Brief: Induced Abortion," *The Alan Guttmacher Institute*, 1998, <http://www.agi-usa.org>

6. Carl Weiser, "Bill to Be Introduced to Stop Minors From Crossing State Lines for Abortions," *Gannett News Service*, February 1, 1998, p. arc. (March 20, 1998).

7. "What is Medical Abortion?," *The National Abortion Federation*, 1997, <http://www.prochoice.org> (March 13, 1998).

8. Freedom of Access to Clinic Entrances Act of 1994.

9. Kali Wallace, "There's More to the Abortion Debate than the Actions of a Few Nutters," *University Wire*, February 20, 1998.

Chapter 6. The Pro-Life Camp

1. Garry Wills, "Nation: 'Save the Babies' Operation Rescue; a Case Study in Galvanizing the Antiabortion Movement," *Time*, May 1, 1989, pp. 26ff.

2. Frederica Mathewes-Green, "Beyond 'it's a baby': If Pro-Lifers Give More Thought to Women's Needs, They Will Serve Children Better . . ." *National Review*, vol. 49, December 31, 1997, pp. 40ff.

3. Wills, pp. 26ff.

4. Joan Lowy, "Dad? Who Needs Him? Support of Non-Traditional Families Send Religious Right into a Tizzy," *Arizona Republic*, August 29, 1999, p. E10.

5. Lennart Nilsson, *A Child is Born* (New York: Dell Publishing, 1993), p. 77.

6. Stephen C. Meyer, "'Fully Formed': the Discoveries of Fetology," *Eternity*, June 1985, page number unavailable.

7. Nilsson, p. 108.

8. Amanda Smith, "'Jane Roe' Spoke at Texas A&M About Her Choices in Life," *University Wire*, February 23, 1998.

9. Mike Feinsilber, "A Woman's Right to Choose," *The Columbian*, January 18, 1998, p. A3.

10. "Abortion and the Republicans: Idealists v. Realists, *The Economist*, vol. 346, January 24, 1998, electronic library download.

11. Ibid.

Chapter 7. Other Choices

1. Margaret Carlson, "Partial-Truth Abortion," *Time*, March 24, 1997.

2. "Facts in Brief: Teen Sex & Pregnancy," *The Allen Guttmacher Institute*, 1996, <http://www.agi-usa.org> (March 20, 1998).

3. Ibid.

4. "Facts in Brief: Induced Abortion," *The Alan Guttmacher Institute*, 1998, <http://www.agi-usa.org> (March 20, 1998).

5. Charles C. Haynes, "Finding Common Ground: A Phone Network Seeks to Close Abortion Issue Schism," *Gannett News Service*, November 3, 1997, pp. arc.

6. Ibid.

7. Elizabeth Gleick and Giovanna Breu, "Controversy: Bridging Troubled Waters While the Abortion furor Rages, Former Adversaries Find Common Ground," *People*, August 31, 1992, p. 77.

8. Ibid.

9. Linda Feldmann, "Bridging the Abortion Divide One Discussion at a Time," *The Christian Science Monitor*, January 21, 1998, p. 1.

Andryszewski, Tricia. *Abortion: Rights, Options, and Choices*. Brookfield, Conn.: Millbrook Press, Inc., 1996.

Gold, Susan Dudley. *Roe v. Wade*. New York: Twenty-First Century Books, 1995.

Guernsey, JoAnn. *Abortion: Understanding the Controversy*. Minneapolis, Minn.: The Lerner Publishing Group, 1993.

Lowenstein, Felicia. *The Abortion Battle: Looking at Both Sides*. Springfield, N.J.: Enslow Publishers, Inc., 1996.

Nelson, Joan. *Abortion*. San Diego, Calif.: Lucent Books, 1992.

Tompkins, Nancy. *Roe vs. Wade: The Fight Over Life & Liberty*. Danbury, Conn.: Franklin Watts, Inc., 1996.

Further Reading